Loaves of Fun

A HISTORY OF BREAD WITH ACTIVITIES AND RECIPES FROM AROUND THE WORLD

Elizabeth M. Harbison
Illustrated by John Harbison

CHICAGO
REVIEW
PRESS

Library of Congress Cataloging-in-Publication Data

Harbison, Elizabeth M.
    Loaves of fun: a history of bread with activities and recipes from around the
world/Elizabeth M. Harbison; illustrated by John Harbison.—1st ed.
      p. cm.
    Summary: A collection of recipes for various kinds of breads arranged in a
timeline format that the charts the history of this staple food from the earliest civilization to the present day. Includes instructions for related activities.
    ISBN 1-55652-311-4
    1. Bread—History—Juvenile literature. 2. Cookery (Bread)—Juvenile litera-
ture. 3. Cookery, International—Juvenile literature. [1. Bread. 2. Baking.] I. Harbison,
John, 1950- ill. II. Title.
TX769.H294 1997
641.8'15—dc21   96-47311
                                                      CIP
                                                      AC

©1997 by Elizabeth M. Harbison
Illustrations ©1997 by John Harbison
All rights reserved
First edition
Published by Chicago Review Press, Incorporated
814 N. Franklin Street
Chicago, IL 60610
5 4 3 2 1

Acknowledgments

Thanks to Tom and Mary McMakin and the whole Great Harvest Bakery family. Your breads are an inspiration to me and, fortunately, to Amy Teschner, who thought of this book and saw it through its beginning stages.

Thanks to Olivia Nuccio, who modeled for everything from kneading hands to the eating mummy.

This book is lovingly dedicated to my own little tester and helper, Mary Paige Harbison.

CONTENTS

INTRODUCTION

This book is about the history of bread. But what you might not know is that the history of bread is also the history of civilization.

Reading this book will be like taking a trip through history and throughout the world. You'll learn how important bread has been in the making and breaking of civilizations, both ancient and modern.

Virtually every culture in history has had its own approach to eating, from the Chinese way of eating with chopsticks and the Moroccan way of eating with the left hand, to the European invention of utensils: knives, forks, and spoons.

The favorite foods of different cultures also vary greatly: in Greece, squid is popular; in India, beef is forbidden; in France, frogs' legs and snails are considered delicious; and in Italy, pasta is served nearly every night.

The one thing that's common to virtually every culture in every period of history is that all of them have or have had some kind of bread with nearly every meal. But the kinds of bread vary as greatly as the cultures themselves. You can see evidence of this in the French baguette, the Jewish challah, the Indian chapati, and the Middle Eastern pita, to name just a few.

If there's anything the recipes in this book teach you, I hope it's that you can experiment freely in the kitchen and try different ingredients. That's how the Romans—and the civilizations that followed—went from having plain wheat bread to having many of the same fruit and nut breads you find in the bakery and grocery store today. Sometimes you might end up with something that doesn't taste very good, but I'll bet that more often than not you'll love your own bread creations and your family and friends will, too.

Enjoy!

KITCHEN AND COOKING TIPS

Safety

1. The kitchen is a pretty safe place, but it's not a place to play. There are certain things you must be very careful of: all utensils, especially knives; electrical appliances and outlets, including mixers and toasters (never, ever put anything metal in a toaster!); cleaning solutions, which are often stored under the kitchen sink; and anything else that looks like it might fall on you, cut you, or shock you.

2. Never use the oven or stove without a grown-up's permission and help. Fires can start before you know it, and it's important to have someone with you who can handle an emergency. You'll need an adult for all the recipes and activities in this book.

3. Make sure you have a fire extinguisher and/or a big, open box of baking soda handy in case there is a fire (baking soda will put the fire out if you pour it on).

Baking Tips

1. The best way to mix bread dough is with your hands. Not only is this the safest way, but it's also the most fun. Use a large bowl. Throw all the ingredients in according to the directions and mix them up with your hands (make sure you wash them first!).

2. Measuring ingredients is also really easy. All you need is a measuring cup and a measuring spoon (or a collection of measuring spoons of different sizes). Before long, you may be able to measure ingredients just by pouring them into your palm or into a cup. You can practice this by measuring an ingredient with a measuring spoon or cup first, then pouring it into your hand (if it's a small amount of dry ingredient, like salt or yeast) or into a coffee cup or glass. Soon you'll learn what a tablespoon of sugar looks like in your hand and you won't have to get out the measuring spoons at all!

3. Never use ingredients that smell or look different than you know they should. Flour can grow rancid and turn brown, milk can curdle, eggs can rot, and weevils (tiny bugs) can burrow into flour and sugar if they're not stored properly.

4. It's a good idea to "proof" your yeast before you use it, just to make sure it's alive and active so you don't end up with a big hard pancake instead of a loaf of bread.

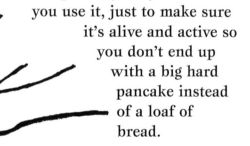

To proof yeast, simply stir some sugar into a cup of very warm but not hot water (you should be able to put a finger in it comfortably) and sprinkle a little yeast on top. It doesn't matter how much yeast you use; a pinch will do. Within five minutes, the yeast should start to bubble or foam. If it doesn't, it's not fresh enough to use.

5. All of the recipes in this book call for butter, but you can use margarine if you prefer.

Six slices of bread equals up to one-third of the vitamins and minerals you need in a whole day!

Notes on Kneading

When all the ingredients for bread dough are mixed, you're ready to knead. Kneading is easy, and everyone has their own way of doing it. You can't go wrong. All you have to do is pull the dough apart and then squish it back together again, over and over. Some people like to do this by making the dough into a flat circle and folding it over like a pillowcase again and again. Others prefer to pull it like taffy, stretching it out and then mushing it into a ball before stretching it out again. The idea of kneading is to stretch the protein in the dough. You should knead for at least ten minutes, but don't worry: you can't do too much. Whatever is the most fun is the right way to do it.

It's best to put all of the ingredients together first and save the kneading to go with the last additions of flour. It almost always works out this way because bread dough tends to be sticky until you knead in just the right amount of flour. If the dough is coming off on your fingers when you pull your hand away, you know that you need to work in a little more flour. Add a tablespoon or so at a time until you have a smooth, elastic loaf that is easy to pull and fold but isn't wet.

If your dough gets too tough and you have a difficult time pulling it apart, add a little bit of water (about one teaspoon) and work it into the dough until you have the proper consistency. You might have to add water a couple of times in order to get it just right.

After you've done it a few times, you won't have any trouble at all knowing just what the perfect dough feels like.

Materials

Here's a list of all the materials you'll need to make every recipe in this book. This list may look long, but most kitchens already have these things.

Shallow baking pan
Bread knife
Cookie sheet
Dish towel
Drinking glass
Large frying pan or skillet
Medium frying pan
Sharp knife

Loaf pan, 9 x 5 x 2½ inches
Set of measuring cups
Set of measuring spoons
Large mixing bowl
Plastic mixing bowl
Pastry brush
Medium plastic bowl with cover
Rolling pin
Large non-aluminum saucepan
Metal spatula
Two-quart saucepan
Long-handled spoon
Wooden stirring spoon
Whisk or fork to beat eggs

Measuring Equivalents

1 tablespoon = 3 teaspoons
2 tablespoons = 1 ounce
$\frac{1}{4}$ cup = 4 tablespoons or 12 teaspoons
1 cup = 8 ounces
1 stick of butter = 8 tablespoons
1 pinch = $\frac{1}{4}$ teaspoon
1 package of yeast = 1 scant tablespoon

A TIMELINE HISTORY OF BREAD

Bread began as a lumpy, oatmeal-like substance. It was a crude mixture of ground grain and water, two things that were readily available in any part of the world at any time of the year.

This mixture wasn't really bread, and wouldn't become so until people started baking it between 4000 and 2000 B.C. But this oatmealy mush is important because it shows that as long as 75,000 years ago, the people of Asia had put together the two most basic ingredients of bread—mushed grain and water. Archaeologists have found flattened stones that were clearly made to crush grain and have been able to date those stone tools back to 73,000 B.C.

Even though Asia is the cradle of breadmaking technology, people in modern Asia consume very little bread. In China rice cakes (crunchy rounds of puffed rice) are popular, but they aren't really bread in the way we know it.

Also, China and Japan make rice flour (called *mochi* in Japanese), but it's used primarily to thicken sauces and make desserts. Since rice flour has no gluten, it cannot be used to make raised (leavened) bread unless it's mixed with a high-gluten flour like most wheat flours.

ASIA

By 8000 B.C. (about 10,000 years ago) people were mixing crushed grain with water and heating it over a fire, which is a lot like modern oatmeal or porridge. Some ancient grains and seeds, still blackened from fires long ago, that got cooked but never eaten have been found by scientists.

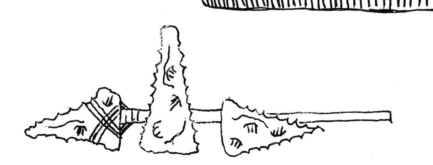

Another Asian country is India. Modern India also doesn't have a lot of bread, but the two most famous Indian breads have been eaten there since the earliest days of their civilization. A *pappadam* is a very thin wafer, sort of like a Mexican tortilla, but made from lentil flour. When pappadams are deep-fried, they puff up. They're served either plain or seasoned with pepper. The other famous Indian bread is the *chapati*, which is an unleavened biscuit made from whole wheat flour and water. It's used mostly for scooping up food from the plate.

MESOPOTAMIA

In ancient Mesopotamia, an area in Asia between the Tigris River and the lower Euphrates River, people lived in the pockets of the Armenian mountain range. This was the earliest civilization, and tools, remains of small homes, and human bones have been found and dated back 6,000 years.

The Mesopotamians were the first to try growing and eating different kinds of grains mixed with water which they baked or boiled over a fire.

SWITZERLAND

In Switzerland, people known as "lake dwellers" left the remains of a village near Geneva. Archaeologists have found bread among the tools and the remains of dwellings. They've also found grains from several different kinds of wheat. This is important because it is the earliest record of bread in Europe, a place now famous for its many different varieties of bread.

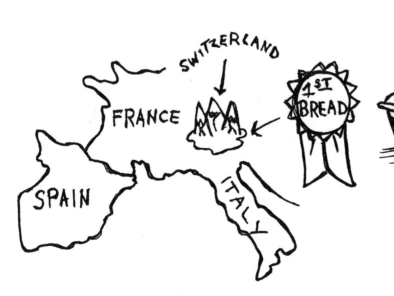

HOW CAVEMEN COOKED

The first cooks were prehistoric people. They didn't have really good hunting, cooking, or food storing methods, and fire was a big discovery. Cooking directly over an open fire was about as advanced as their cooking technology got, but boy, was that fire important!

Prehistoric people would put chunks of meat on a stick and hold it directly in the flames. For bread, they mixed grain and water to make a mush that they cooked on rocks heated in the fire.

As time passed and civilizations became more advanced, people eventually learned to make very basic ovens in which to cook their bread. The early Romans really took this idea seriously, and practically everyone in ancient Rome had an oven of some sort.

After that, ovens didn't change very much until the invention of the electric oven in the early 1900s. Until then, ovens were all boxes (of various sizes and made out of various things) that were heated by fire.

Drop Biscuits

HERE'S WHAT YOU'LL NEED:

2 cups flour

2 teaspoons baking powder

1 teaspoon baking soda

4 tablespoons (½ stick) butter, softened, plus extra for greasing

¾ cup milk

This is a very simple type of bread which could have been made easily in an oven box. Biscuit mix (like Bisquick) makes really good biscuits and is faster and easier than making them from scratch, but if you want real buttery drop biscuits, this is the recipe.

HERE'S WHAT YOU'LL DO:

1. Heat the oven to 450°F and grease the bottom of a baking pan.
2. Place all the ingredients in a large bowl and mix them with your clean hands until you have a smooth batter with no big lumps of flour.
3. Drop small handfuls of biscuit dough (a little bit bigger than a golf ball) onto the greased baking pan.
4. Bake 10 minutes or until golden brown on top.

Makes 12 biscuits

UNLEAVENED BREAD

Another name for those earliest breads is unleavened bread. Unleavened bread is flat, dense bread that hasn't risen with yeast or soda. Before the discovery of yeast all breads were unleavened. There aren't as many varieties of unleavened bread as there are of yeast, batter, and quick breads, but some unleavened breads are still popular today.

The best-known unleavened bread is *matzo*, which Jewish people eat every year during Passover.

One of the most ancient unleavened breads—Arabian pita bread—is still popular today. This comes from the Middle East, where it has been eaten for centuries. Today there are many brands of pita bread available,

and they're made out of all sorts of different grains, like oatmeal, whole wheat, and rye. You can recognize pita bread pretty easily because it is round and, when you slice it in half, you find a "pocket." This makes sandwich making easy—all you do is drop your sandwich fixings in and voila! Instant sandwich.

Another way people eat pita bread is by cutting it into triangles and toasting them until they're crisp. Then they're eaten plain or are dipped into a sauce like hummus, which is made from chickpeas, lemon juice, sesame paste, salt, and pepper—it's delicious and nutritious!

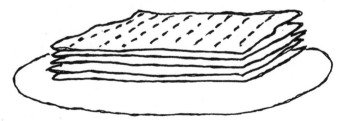

Pita Bread

HERE'S WHAT YOU'LL NEED:

- 1½ cups all-purpose flour
- 1 cup whole wheat flour
- 1 teaspoon (almost ½ package) yeast (optional)
- 1 tablespoon sugar
- 1 teaspoon salt
- 2 tablespoons olive oil
- 1 egg
- 1 cup water

HERE'S WHAT YOU'LL DO:

1. Combine all the ingredients in a mixing bowl and make a firm, smooth dough. Let it sit for 1 hour undisturbed.
2. Heat the oven to broil or 550°F. Divide the dough into eight equal balls. Put them on a cookie sheet and press or roll each ball into a very flat disk.
3. Bake for 4–5 minutes in the hot oven or until lightly toasted. Remove quickly when they're ready or else they'll burn.
4. Eat!

Makes 8 pita pockets

Traditional pita was made without any leavener, but I find my pita pockets are just a little bit better and easier to make if I add about a teaspoon of yeast.

Hummus is a delicious dip for pita bread. People have been eating this combination since the earliest Middle Eastern civilizations.

To make hummus, all you have to do is put 1 cup of drained, canned chickpeas (also called garbanzo beans) into a blender or food processor. If you have dried beans, soak them overnight to soften them, then drain them. Add ¼ cup tahini sesame paste (in the international section of your grocery store), ¼ cup olive oil, 3 peeled garlic cloves, and 1 tablespoon lemon juice. Process this mixture until smooth, then dip torn pita bread in and enjoy!

This is not only delicious, but it's very, very good for you.

Ancient Egypt is where bread really began to take shape as the yeasty food we enjoy today. The Egyptians made all sorts of improvements to bread making, like harvesting grain, milling it, and—most importantly—adding yeast.

Egyptian drawings found in the tombs of pharaohs actually show pictures of people milling grain and baking bread! Because of this message left by people thousands of years ago, we know that they considered bread a very important part of life.

Early Egyptians figured out that the grain they gathered came from seeds that came from the grasses. They dug up the earth on

either side of the Nile River and scattered the seeds over the wet soil. Their harvests included wheat (which they called *emmer*) and barley. In order to harvest their grains, the ancient Egyptians made sickles out of sharpened flint and mounted them on wooden sticks. These were the perfect instruments for chopping down the tall grasses.

After cutting they put all the stalks of wheat together and had cattle walk on the grasses to separate the grain from the blade. The grain was the only part they wanted for cooking. Then they scooped up the grain and used special bowls to toss it in the air and catch it again. This is called winnowing, and it removed the hard, inedible outside covering of the grain, called the chaff. It was then time to mill, or grind, the grain down to a powder by mashing it between two hard, flat rocks called millstones.

After the grain was milled, it was transferred to baskets. A scribe counted and recorded the number of baskets before they were transferred to the granary where the grain was stored.

The ancient Egyptian families grew or raised all of the foods they ate on their own property or on the estate they lived on. Once it was prepared, they stored their water and food in large pottery jars and baskets.

In Thebes, Egypt, a basket of bread that was baked 3,500 years ago was found recently. Thanks to the hot, dry climate of Egypt the

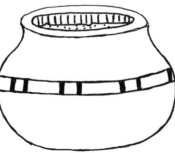

bread was well preserved and still looked much like it must have when it was first baked those thousands of years ago.

Bread has also been found in the tombs of Egyptian pharaohs. When a pharaoh died he was buried with many things that people thought he would need in the afterlife—things like gold, jewelry, clothing, furniture, pictures, and blankets. The Egyptians also buried bread in the shape of servants with these kings because it was thought that they would need servants in the afterlife, too.

All of this is proof that bread was very, very important to the ancient Egyptians. In fact, they had more than forty different kinds of bread. Part of the reason the ancient Egyptians were able to have so many different kinds of bread is that they were the first to make what we call leavened, or raised, bread. This is the fluffy, chewy bread that we all think of now when we think of bread. Before the Egyptians came along and used yeast in bread, all bread was hard and flat.

No one knows exactly how or why yeast was first used in bread. But there are two interesting stories about it.

The first story is that there was once a baker who hired a very clumsy boy to help him bake breads. This boy was always knocking things over, tripping, and running into things.

One day while the baker was hurrying to make some bread for the pharaoh, the clumsy boy knocked a bottle of ale into the bread dough. Since the baker was in a hurry and didn't have time to mix a whole new dough, he added a little more flour to the dough and mixed it.

Since ale contains yeast, the dough started to expand, like a balloon. The baker watched in amazement for a couple of hours as the bread dough grew larger and larger. When he finally baked it, the resulting loaf was tall and wide and as light as air. The pharaoh loved it, and soon everyone in the land was pouring ale into their bread dough to make the fancy raised bread.

The other story about how leavened bread came about is not about a clumsy baker's assistant but about a lazy baker.

This baker had lots of bread to bake, but halfway through the job he ran out of water. He was so lazy that he couldn't bear the idea of finding his water bucket and going into the town center to fill it, so instead he used the only other liquid he had in the place—his ale.

This wasn't an easy choice for the lazy baker because he really liked to relax with a bit of ale in the afternoons. Finally, though, his laziness won out and he poured the ale into the bread dough.

Then he sat down to rest. After all, making that decision had taken a lot of energy out of him. So he sat, and he fell asleep. When he woke up, he saw that the bread had risen to twice its previous size. He took this as a sign that the gods were rewarding him for his goodness, and he baked the bread.

When he took the bread out of the fire, he saw that it had risen even a little bit more. He was so pleased that he told everyone in his village about the fluffy bread made with ale. Soon everyone was baking their bread with ale instead of water.

Whichever story is true, we do know one thing: raised bread was discovered in ancient Egypt and has been made ever since.

Even though the ancient Egyptian bread was yeast bread, the Egyptians didn't have little envelopes of yeast the way we do today. Instead, they made a yeast sponge. That is, they left a little piece of the dough out each time they baked a loaf so that they could use it as a starter for the next loaf. In between baking, they left their starters sitting out so that the yeast that floats around in the air naturally would get into it.

The tradition of using a sponge or starter has had a big role in almost every civilization since ancient Egypt. Recipes for sponges have been passed down for thousands of years since then. Until recently, people were completely dependent upon a sponge in order to make bread.

TWO WAYS TO MAKE A SOURDOUGH SPONGE

Sourdough sponge, or starter, is the thing that makes sourdough bread rise into a tall, fluffy loaf. Without it, the bread would be hard and flat like a hockey puck.

A sponge is a thick liquid, very much like cake batter. The most important thing to remember is that it must be kept fresh, which is done by using it. In the old days, it was easy to keep it fresh because bread was baked from it several times a week.

Today, if you don't use your sponge to make bread at least once a week, you still have to "feed" it; that is, take a cup of it out, throw it away (or better yet give it to a friend or relative), and replace the discarded cup with one cup of flour and one cup of milk or water.

Old-Fashioned Sourdough Sponge

This sponge works by attracting the yeast spores that float around in the air naturally, so you don't want to cover this concoction while it sits on the counter. This recipe works best in a place where there is lots of yeast in the air to start with, like in a bakery or kitchen.

HERE'S WHAT YOU'LL NEED:

1 cup active-culture buttermilk (it says "active culture" on the carton)

1 cup flour

HERE'S WHAT YOU'LL DO:

1. Leave the buttermilk out in an uncovered glass for 24 hours.
2. In a bowl, stir the milk and the flour. Let the mixture sit in a warm place (maybe near the oven) for 4–5 days. Stir it once a day.
3. When it gets bubbly and smells sour, it's ready to use!
4. Transfer the mixture to a covered container and refrigerate. Every time you use 1 cup of it, add 1 cup ordinary milk and 1 cup flour, stir, and leave it out in a warm place for 1 day before returning it to the refrigerator.

Makes one 2-cup sponge

1 tablespoon (1 package) yeast

2 cups bread flour

2 cups lukewarm milk

HERE'S WHAT YOU'LL DO:

1. Combine the yeast, flour, and milk in a bowl and mix well.
2. Pour the mixture into a covered container and leave it out in a warm place for 5 days. Shake or stir it once a day.
3. The starter is now ready to use. Every time you take 1 cup out (either to make bread or keep the starter alive) feed the starter by adding 1 cup flour and 1 cup milk or water (alternate each time). After feeding, let the starter sit out for 1 day, then store it in the refrigerator until the next time you use it. Follow the pattern of feeding, leaving out 1 day, then refrigerating every time you use it.

Makes one 4-cup starter

Modern Sourdough Starter

Since you're adding yeast to this sponge yourself, you can cover the container while it sits out.

Important Notes on Your Sourdough Sponge

If the sponge changes color, throw it out and start over.

If your sponge develops a very foul odor, throw it out.

Remember to use the sponge and feed it at least once a week. If you don't make bread with it, just throw 1 cup away and stir in 1 cup flour and 1 cup liquid (either milk or water).

While the sponge is being stored in the refrigerator, stir or shake it every few days.

Your sponge may be frozen for up to 1 month and thawed gently in the refrigerator.

Sponges can be used in any bread recipe if you reduce the other liquids in the recipe by one-third for every cup of sponge you use.

Remember: when you treat your sourdough sponge properly, it will last forever.

Sourdough Bread

Here's a recipe that works perfectly with your sourdough sponge.

HERE'S WHAT YOU'LL NEED:

1 cup sourdough starter (see previous recipes)

3 cups bread flour

2 tablespoons sugar

2 teaspoons salt

2 tablespoons butter, plus extra for greasing

$2/3$ cup milk

HERE'S WHAT YOU'LL DO:

1. Combine all the ingredients in a bowl and mix to make a smooth, elastic ball.
2. Knead the dough on a lightly floured counter for 10 minutes. Place the dough in a greased bowl and cover lightly with a dish towel.
3. Let the dough rise for 2 hours or until it doubles in bulk.
4. Punch the dough down and let it rest for 15 minutes.
5. Transfer the dough into a greased loaf pan and let it rise for another $1\frac{1}{2}$ hours. After $1\frac{1}{4}$ hours, heat the oven to 375°F.
6. Bake for 50 minutes or until it sounds hollow when you knock on it.

Makes 1 loaf

A BIT ABOUT YEAST

Most of the bread you see and eat today is yeast bread. As you might guess, that means it's made with yeast. It also means that when you make it, it's necessary to knead it, or stretch and pull on it for a certain amount of time in order to stretch out the sticky protein called gluten. While other breads might use a yeast or yeast sponge, actual yeast bread is characterized by the necessity to knead it.

Yeast is a living, single-cell organism that "eats" sugar and converts it to carbon dioxide gas. In other words, sugar goes into the yeast but comes right back out as gas. This gas blows bubbles into the bread dough and makes it grow bigger (just like a balloon grows when you blow it up or your bubble gum gets bigger when you blow a bubble). Recipes almost always call for sugar or honey or some other sweetener since that is what yeast likes best.

Recipes also call for salt. This is because salt slows down the production of all those little gas bubbles so that the bread doesn't get too big. It also makes the bread taste good.

There are three kinds of yeast that you can use for breadmaking. They are:

1. *Compressed fresh yeast*, which comes in little damp cakes that crumble easily in your hand. Many people feel that this yeast gives the best flavor. Because it's so fresh, the bread you make with it lasts longer on the counter . . . but it also tastes so good that you'll eat it quickly. Compressed yeast must be refrigerated and lives only a couple of weeks.

2. *Active dry yeast* comes in either jars or envelopes. One envelope contains a little less than one tablespoon, and usually three envelopes are sealed together. These envelopes are sealed tight so no air gets in. As a result, the yeast is alive but dormant (sort of sleeping) until it is revived in warm liquid. Unopened packages of active dry yeast may last six to ten months. Active dry yeast makes good-tasting bread, but a lot of people prefer bread made with compressed yeast. Bread made with active dry yeast will last fairly long on the counter.

3. *Quick rising yeast* comes in envelopes like active dry yeast and is sometimes called rapid rise yeast. It's used in the same way as active dry yeast, but it works in about half the time! This is good for really impatient people—especially if they're impatient to eat, because bread made with quick rising yeast only lasts a couple of days before it starts to go stale.

Blow Up a Balloon with Yeast

HERE'S WHAT YOU'LL NEED:

1 balloon

1 tablespoon (1 package) yeast

¼ cup sugar or honey

1 cup very warm water, plus extra for filling a mixing bowl

1 liter-sized plastic soda bottle, cleaned and dry

1 piece of string or 1 rubber band

HERE'S WHAT YOU'LL DO:

1. Stretch the balloon by blowing it up and letting the air out a couple of times (this is a little bit like kneading).
2. Stir the yeast, sugar or honey, and 1 cup warm water together, and pour it into the plastic soda bottle.
3. Put the balloon completely over the opening of the bottle, and hold it in place with string or a rubber band.

This experiment will show you that yeast really does blow out gas when it's mixed with sugar, even though you can't actually see the gas. When you mix sugar and water in a bottle and then cover it with a balloon, the gas will rise into the balloon and blow it up. If the yeast and sugar were in bread dough rather than the bottle, the gas would blow up the loaf instead of the balloon.

4. Fill a mixing bowl or pot halfway with warm water and put the soda bottle in it.
5. The yeast will make the water in the soda bottle bubble and foam, and watch—like magic the gas will blow up the balloon!

NOW, BACK TO THE ANCIENT EGYPTIANS . . .

Another reason the Egyptians had so many varieties of bread was because they added things other than flour, water, salt, and leavener. They also made breads flavored with fruit, garlic, and various kinds of nuts. To prepare bread, they mixed their dough in a clay bowl, then set the bowl on the fire to bake it. All of the mixing and baking was done in this one bowl without ever taking it out. This operation is like the modern-day bread machine, which mixes and bakes all in one bowl within the machine.

The Egyptians considered baking to be a form of art. The Greeks later referred to them as *artophagoi*, which means "the bread eaters."

We'll be getting to the Greeks in a moment.

1400 B.C.
EGYPT

Around 1400 B.C. the Jews couldn't stand living lives of slavery in Egypt any longer, and they decided to leave. This is referred to as the Exodus.

The story is that they left so quickly that they didn't have enough time to bring along most of their things, including their bread starter, which they saved at home.

Because they didn't have leavener, the Jews had to bake bread without it. This ended up as a flat, crisp bread called matzo, which is still eaten in the eight-day celebration of Passover.

Passover is only one example of how bread is often used in religious celebrations. Because bread was the main food in past civilizations, it became important in many religions as well. In ancient Rome, ovens were often built into temples. During Roman Catholic mass, bread is torn and eaten as a symbol of the body of Jesus Christ.

RED SEA

Challah Braid

Challah (pronounced HA-la) is a traditional Jewish egg bread. It's very tender and tasty, and when you make it into a braid, it's an impressive thing to look at, too!

HERE'S WHAT YOU'LL NEED:

Bread

2 tablespoons (2 packages) yeast

3 cups bread flour

2 tablespoons sugar

2 teaspoons salt

3 tablespoons butter

2 eggs

1 cup water

Glaze

1 egg

1 teaspoon sugar

Poppy seeds, for sprinkling

HERE'S WHAT YOU'LL DO:

1. To make the bread, mix all the ingredients except the glaze ingredients in a large bowl to make a smooth, elastic dough.
2. Turn the dough out on a floured counter and knead it for 10 minutes.
3. Return the dough to a bowl and cover it with a dish towel. Leave it to rise for 1 hour. Then punch it down and let it rest for 15 minutes.
4. Divide the dough into three equal parts and roll them into thick logs. Put them on a cookie sheet and join them all at the top. Then braid them down to the bottom, just like you would your hair.
5. Cover the bread braid with a dish cloth and let it rise in a warm place for 45 minutes.
6. To make the glaze, heat the oven to 375°F. Beat the egg and 1 teaspoon sugar together and brush over the braid with a pastry brush. Before it dries, sprinkle with poppy seeds.
7. Bake for 45 minutes or until the top is lightly browned.
8. Serve the bread warm or cool.

Makes 1 challah loaf

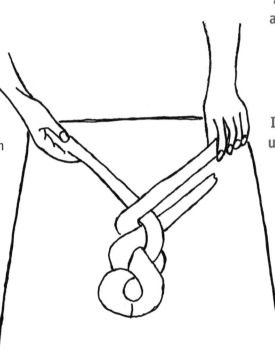

The three strands of a challah braid represent the ropes used to hang Haman, who was the prime minister of the ancient civilization of Ahasuerus. Haman hated the Jews and did many awful things to them in ancient Persia. He was finally stopped, and to this day Jews celebrate the end of his terrifying reign.

In those days, salt was customarily used in all sacrifices. Today, challah is dipped in salt before eating to commemorate the sacrificial custom.

GREECE

It seems to be around 800 B.C., or 2,800 years ago, that the Greeks began baking bread. We think that they learned about it from the Egyptians, since old Grecian texts refer to the Egyptians as "bread eaters."

Everything archaeologists have learned indicates that the ancient Greeks enjoyed bread. They ate simply, only two meals a day, and these meals usually consisted of bread, fruit, vegetables, and wine. But the Greeks didn't go very far in creating new breads.

However, they told the Romans (in next-door Italy) about bread, and they took it very seriously.

ROME

In ancient Rome, bread baking became a real art. Bread was the staple of all of Roman meals, but the Romans enjoyed variety and so people specialized in becoming bakers to provide this valued food.

Because of the Roman fondness for breads, bakers were among the highest members of society. All of them tried to outdo each other by thinking of new kinds of breads, new shapes for bread, and new meals to go with the breads. The rest of the people waited eagerly to find out what they would come up with next. As a result, these highly regarded bakers hobnobbed with the wealthiest class.

The first large-quantity milling processes were invented in ancient Rome. Grinding grain with two handheld rocks took a very long time. It took a lot of work to make even a little bit of bread. The Romans created mills that were powered by wind and water, so they could grind a lot more grain with one single mill—and no blisters on their fingers!

The Romans also invented the first ovens. Clay pots held over a fire weren't very practical for baking huge amounts of bread at a time, so they created ovens made from dried and hardened mud. The mud was fired repeatedly, the way pottery is, until it was very solid and hard. Then the ovens were set in the walls of buildings and heated by fire.

Bread was also an important part of the first welfare system. Because there were many poor people starving, the Roman government created a simple form of bread called *annona* and distributed it to the poor in the streets.

This is not the only instance of a country's government getting involved to make sure the people had bread. Centuries later in France, the government controlled the prices on bread to ensure that every person would be able to afford it.

French bakers were not thrilled with this policy because it meant less money for them, so they tried to figure out a way to make bread into something other than, well, bread. So they experimented with adding sugars, like chocolate and icing. The result? Pastry!

Anyone could eat bread but only the rich could afford to have the fancy pastries. Pretty soon, pastries and cakes became the ultimate symbol of wealth in France. (You'll learn more about this when we get to Marie Antoinette.)

To this day, the French are famous for their rich, delicious pastries.

ROME

Once the milling process worked on large quantities of grain, the ancient Romans began opening bakery stores. By 200 B.C. (2,100 years ago) there were more than two hundred of these commercial bakeries in Rome, and the bakers were so highly respected that lots of people wanted to become one.

ROME

Between A.D. 63 and 79 the Romans grew used to their wind- and water-powered mills and wanted still more convenience. They invented a water-powered mill that had gears and other advanced features so that they could control exactly how fast the grinding went and how fine the powdered flour was when it came out.

The Romans also began making food dishes that used bread as an ingredient, rather than simply making and eating bread alone. A man named Apicius wrote a cookbook called *The Art of Cooking*. As far as we know, this was the first cookbook ever published.

ROME

In A.D. 100 the first school for bakers was opened in Rome. This made it easier for people to learn about the art of baking bread, but it was still only one school and it wasn't as easy back then for people all over the country to travel hundreds of miles to attend school as it is now. So outside the city, bread baking was still thought of as a mysterious process.

Roman Bread Pudding

This is a recipe from Apicius's book, *The Art of Cooking*. Of course, here it's modified for you to use in your own kitchen today.

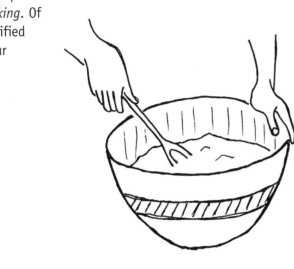

HERE'S WHAT YOU'LL NEED:

1/2 cup milk

2 thick slices bread

1/4 cup olive oil, any type

Honey, to taste

HERE'S WHAT YOU'LL DO:

1. Pour the milk into a mixing bowl.
2. Rip the bread into bite-sized pieces and soak them in the milk. Move them around to make sure each piece has the same amount of milk soaked into it.
3. In a frying pan, heat the olive oil over medium-high heat.
4. Put the milk-soaked bread into the frying pan and fry until golden brown on each side.
5. Drizzle with honey and serve.

Makes 2 servings

EUROPE

The stories aren't clear on where the pretzel was invented, but one story says that in the early Middle Ages, there was once a priest who loved children. This priest was also a bread baker, and one day he had an idea about a treat to make to amuse the children of his village.

He made his bread dough, but instead of forming it into loaves, he rolled it into ropes and twisted them together into the shape of praying hands. This shape was so popular that we still eat "prayer bread" today—it's called pretzels!

Those first pretzels were not hard, crunchy, and salted but soft and chewy. Nowadays we can get both kinds, but back then the hot, soft kind were the only ones available.

Then, as now, they were a favorite of children.

Pretzels

You can make pretzels that are very much like the ones made by the priest who invented them. Eat them plain or salted, or dip them in mustard.

HERE'S WHAT YOU'LL NEED:

2 teaspoons (¾ package) yeast

3 cups unbleached white flour

1 tablespoon sugar

½ teaspoon salt

2 tablespoons butter, plus extra for greasing

1 cup water, plus 8 cups for boiling

5 teaspoons baking soda

Coarse salt (optional)

HERE'S WHAT YOU'LL DO:

1. Mix the yeast, flour, sugar, salt, 2 tablespoons butter, and 1 cup water together in a large bowl with your hands. Fold the dough over and over again, until it's smooth and firm. If it's too sticky, add a little bit of flour; if it's too tough, add a tiny bit of water. The dough is ready when it doesn't stick to your hands too much.

2. Divide the ready dough into twelve equal parts. Roll each part into a long snake, as you would with play dough. Make each snake into an "O" and twist the ends at the top together several times, then pull them down to touch the bottom of the "O." Do they look like pretzels now? Do they look at least sort of like pretzels? Good.

3. Set the pretzels on a cookie sheet and cover them with a dish cloth. Let them rise in a warm, draft-free place for 45 minutes. Heat the oven to 475°F.

4. Put 4 cups water and 5 teaspoons baking soda in a large non-aluminum saucepan and bring it to a light boil. As soon as the water boils, turn the heat down to low and drop in the pretzels three or four at a time to cook for 1 minute.

5. Take the pretzels out of the water with a spoon, and set them on greased cookie sheets. If you want, sprinkle them with coarse salt.

6. Bake for 10–12 minutes or until browned.

7. Eat!

Makes 12 pretzels

SCANDINAVIA

The Vikings were from Scandinavia (Norway, Sweden, and Denmark). Back then, as now, they had very hard winters with short days, few hours of daylight, and very long cold months. During the summer, when the days were longer and the weather warm enough to go out in and work the fields, Viking farmers had to work very hard to grow and store enough food for the winter.

As in every other culture, grain was a very important part of the Vikings' lives. They grew wheat, oats, barley, and rye so they could bake bread and make ale. They also used oats to make what we think of today as oatmeal, but they called it porridge. This was a very filling, nutritious meal that didn't cost a lot to make.

The Vikings didn't use dried-mud ovens. They still cooked everything over the fire, though they learned to do it very efficiently. While meat cooked on a spit over the fire, they laid flat rocks around the border of the fire so they could utilize the heat for cooking other foods, like bread.

ENGLAND

During the Middle Ages, most people didn't own their own property. They usually had a section of land on the estate of an overlord. The peasants had to pay the overlord to grind their grain into flour at his mill. They also had to pay to bake their bread in his oven.

In the estate houses of the overlords, huge flat breads known as trenchers were used as plates. People piled their spiced meats and limp vegetables onto them, and afterward they either threw the bread trenchers to the dogs (early hush puppies) or collected them to distribute to the poor in the villages.

It wasn't hard to do the dishes in those days!

Around A.D. 1000, the English, following the cue of the French, started serving pastry. Because sugar was so difficult to get (and therefore very expensive), pastry was only for the very rich. The peasants continued to eat oatmeal mixed with water, and occasionally they had some of the hard bread trenchers that the wealthy used to serve food upon.

It's interesting to know that the words *lord* and *lady*, which remain titles for the aristocrats in Great Britain, actually relate to bread.

In Old English the words were *hlaford* and *hlaefdigge*. *Hlaford* means "bread keeper" and eventually became the word *lord*. *Hlaefdigge* means "bread mixer" or "bread kneader," and eventually became the word *lady*. Old English is a language that you wouldn't recognize or be able to understand today even though it's the base of our English language.

Bread Bowls for Soup

HERE'S WHAT YOU'LL NEED:

For each bowl, the heel, or end, of a loaf of crusty bread

Warm soup, any kind

HERE'S WHAT YOU'LL DO:

1. With a bread knife, cut each heel to be about 5 inches long.
2. Scoop the bread out of the inside of the heel, leaving the crust and about ¾ inch of bread. It should look something like a bowl. Set it on a plate.
3. Carefully pour or ladle warm soup into the bread bowl.
4. That's it! Eat!

These bowls are not only fun to eat from, but they're fun to eat afterward! Using bread bowls for soup then eating the bread is a lot like eating off trenchers the way people did in the Middle Ages.

   Make sure you use a very sturdy, crusty bread for these. Otherwise, the bowls will get very soggy. You can use any type of soup with these bowls, but thick soups like cream of broccoli, cheese chowder, or stew work best.

On average, medieval peasants ate two pounds of bread every day!

AMERICA

When the Pilgrims came over from England they had something called ship's biscuits. These were very hard pieces of round bread made from pea flour, wheat flour, and water. They were about the size of dinner plates, but flat so that they were easily stacked in the ships' galleys. They were made before leaving the English shores and were meant to last the entire trip, but the problem was that the biscuits sat so long that they became infested with weevils and maggots. Unfortunately, they were just about all the Pilgrims had to eat, so many of the people waited until after dark to eat so that they wouldn't have to look at what they were eating.

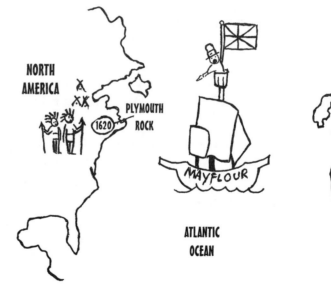

NORTH AMERICA

1620

PLYMOUTH ROCK

MAYFLOUR

ATLANTIC OCEAN

ENGLAND

Once in a while (but not often because it was dangerous onboard) the Pilgrims were able to use fireboxes—iron boxes filled with hot sand—for cooking. One of the best things they made was a thick green pea soup flavored with salted beef or pork. The soup was called *labscouse*. This was about the only time ship's biscuits were good—because the Pilgrims were able to soak the hard bread in the hot soup to soften it up. Also, they were able to soak up every bit of the precious soup with the bread.

Once they arrived in the new world the Pilgrims learned to adapt their cooking habits to the native foods in their new environment. Corn, or *maize*, was one of the most readily available grains, and the Pilgrim women learned to make various kinds of corn breads. When corn bread loaves were served with dinner, they were passed around and everyone simply tore off what they wanted.

Another way the Pilgrims served bread, though, was as plates like the trenchers of the Middle Ages. These bread plates were something like ship's biscuits only softer and without the bugs. The settlers would eat their dinner off the bread plates, then eat the plates.

Corn Bread

 This delicious bread has become an American favorite, particularly with Thanksgiving dinner.

HERE'S WHAT YOU'LL NEED:

4 tablespoons (½ stick) butter, plus extra for greasing

1 cup cornmeal

1 cup flour

1 tablespoon baking powder

1 teaspoon sugar

¼ teaspoon salt

1 cup buttermilk (or 1 cup milk with 1 teaspoon vinegar stirred in)

1 egg

HERE'S WHAT YOU'LL DO:

1. Grease a loaf pan and heat it and the oven to 425°F.
2. Melt the 4 tablespoons butter in the saucepan over low heat, being careful not to let it burn. When it's melted, remove it from the heat.
3. Mix the cornmeal, flour, baking powder, sugar, and salt into a mixing bowl and stir in the melted butter and the buttermilk.
4. Add the egg to the mixture and stir well.
5. Take the hot loaf pan out of the oven and pour the batter in. Return it to the oven and bake for 20 minutes.
6. To tell if it's done, poke a piece of raw spaghetti or a toothpick into the center of the corn bread. If it comes out clean, it's ready. If it comes out with a little batter stuck on it, bake for another 5 minutes and test again.
7. Eat your hot corn bread with your own homemade butter (see next recipe).

Makes 1 loaf

Butter

HERE'S WHAT YOU'LL NEED:

1 cup heavy whipping cream, room temperature

1 jar with a tight-fitting lid

3–4 clean marbles

HERE'S WHAT YOU'LL DO:

1. Pour the heavy cream into the jar, drop the marbles in, and replace the lid tightly.
2. Shake! Keep shaking and the cream will start to form small clumps—this means you're on the right track. Keep shaking and more clumps will form and they'll all stick together until finally you have a large mass of butter at the bottom of your jar with a little bit of liquid on top (the buttermilk). This should take about 20 minutes.

It's easy and fun to make your own butter, and when you serve it on top of your own baked bread, it's even better.

3. Pour the buttermilk off, pick out the marbles, and rinse the butter with water. It's ready to serve!

Makes ¼ cup of butter

Boys and girls of long ago used to make the butter for the family because it was a simple task that didn't require much physical labor. It was, however, a dull task at times, and the children made up rhymes to sing while they did the work.

Here's an old rhyme that you can repeat to yourself while you shake the cream into butter:

Come, butter, come;

Come, butter, come;

Samantha's standing

By the gate,

Waiting for her butter cake.

Come, butter, come.

OTHER BATTER BREADS

Batter breads became popular in Colonial times and have remained part of the American and European diets ever since. Though they often have yeast in them, they're not called yeast bread because they don't need to be kneaded. In other words, yeast breads are made from thick, smooth, elastic dough that you can manipulate with your hands, but batter breads aren't made from dough. Batter breads are made from, well, batter. They don't contain gluten that needs to be stretched by kneading, and often there are eggs in them to help make the bread rise. You use a mixer or wooden spoon to combine the ingredients, not your hands, because the batter is thin and would run through your fingers.

Batter breads also don't need to sit out and rise for any amount of time. You just mix them up and pop them in the oven. Making batter breads is so easy and fast that you might get them confused with quick breads, but we'll discuss those later.

One of the best batter breads is Amish Friendship Bread. It is sweet and wonderful—almost like a cake. It's fun to make because you use a starter sponge and, if you take care of it, every ten days you can give away two new starter sponges.

HERE'S WHAT YOU'LL NEED:

1 cup flour

1 cup sugar

1 cup milk

Pinch of yeast (optional)

HERE'S WHAT YOU'LL DO:

1. Combine the ingredients in a plastic mixing bowl. You don't have to include the yeast, but it might help get things going.
2. Let the mixture sit out uncovered overnight. By morning it should start to bubble because the yeast is releasing carbon dioxide into the mixture.
3. Follow the directions for days 1–10. On the tenth day you'll have two more starter sponges to give away to friends or relatives. Make sure you also include a copy of the instructions and the recipe so that they can take care of their starter and use it to make the same yummy bread you're going to make.

Amish Friendship Bread Starter

After you begin your starter, copy down the instructions and the bread recipe and give them to friends when you give them your leftover starter.

Care and Feeding of Your Amish Friendship Bread Starter

Day 1 Do nothing.

Day 2 Do nothing.

Day 3 Stir with a wooden spoon.

Day 4 Do nothing.

Day 5 Do nothing.

Day 6 Add 1 cup milk, 1 cup sugar, and 1 cup flour. Stir. The lumps will dissolve, so don't worry about them.

Day 7 Do nothing.

Day 8 Stir with a wooden spoon.

Day 9 Do nothing.

Day 10 Add 1 cup milk, 1 cup sugar, and 1 cup flour. Stir. Put 1 cup of the mixture into three different plastic containers. Keep one as your new starter sponge, and give the other two away. There should be some left in the bowl—that's what you make the Amish Friendship Bread with . . . right now!

Amish Friendship Bread

 Your friends and relatives will love this tasty bread. It's especially nice around the holidays.

HERE'S WHAT YOU'LL NEED:

1 cup vegetable oil

½ cup milk

3 eggs

1 teaspoon vanilla extract

1 cup starter

2 cups flour

1 cup sugar

1½ teaspoons baking powder

½ teaspoon baking soda

2 teaspoons cinnamon

½ teaspoon salt

5 ounces (1 large box) instant vanilla pudding

1 cup shelled nuts, any type (optional)

½ cup mixture of cinnamon and sugar

Extra butter, for greasing

HERE'S WHAT YOU'LL DO:

1. Combine the vegetable oil, milk, eggs, vanilla extract, and starter and mix well.
2. Add the flour, sugar, baking powder, baking soda, 2 teaspoons cinnamon, salt, instant pudding, and nuts and stir well.
3. Heat the oven to 325°F and grease two loaf pans.
4. Sprinkle half of the ½ cup cinnamon and sugar mixture into the loaf pans. Pour half of the bread mixture into each pan and top the loaves with the rest of the cinnamon and sugar mixture.
5. Bake for 1 hour, then slide a toothpick into the center of a loaf. If it comes out clean, the bread is ready. If it has some batter stuck to it, cook the bread for another 15 minutes.
6. Serve warm or cool; alone or with a scoop of vanilla ice cream.

Makes 2 loaves

COLONIAL COOKING

Before the invention of the electric oven, it took a lot of ingenuity for people to find ways to cook their bread. Some people used bake kettles, which were iron pots that were suspended on three legs over fire. These were good for baking corn breads and biscuits, as well as meats and soups.

Colonial fireplaces often had ovens built into them. The oven was kept warm because

there was always a fire or hot coals in the fireplace. A common colonial cooking method was to wrap the bread loaves in leaves and set them in hot ashes near the fire. The leaves kept the bread loaves from getting filthy from the ash.

Fireplaces were tremendously large in the old days because they were the only source of heat and light for the home. In most houses, the family slept in

the kitchen as well as cooked and ate there. Many fireplaces had seats built into the sides of the chimneys so that people would always have a place to sit on cold winter nights. Once a week the cook would add kindling and more coals to build a large fire in the kitchen fireplace. This brought the bricks of the fireplace up to a very hot temperature. The coals would reduce to ashes, and then the cook would clean out the ashes and put dried leaves on the hot brick oven floor. Then she would knead some bread dough and set the loaves on long wooden boards called bread peels. Bread peels weren't for baking but rather for setting the bread far back into the hot oven thereby sparing the cook's hands so she didn't burn them by reaching into the oven.

It took all night for those bread loaves to bake, but it was worth it for the family who got to wake up the next morning to hot, fresh bread.

RUSSIA

Between the years of 1650 and 1652, Russia was in crisis. There was lots of rain, and the entire land was flooded for months on end. As a result, none of the crops grew. Without wheat, the people couldn't even make their most basic food—bread. Some books say that the starving people were so desperate that they ate sawdust!

The Russian ruler, the czar, saw his people's desperation and allowed grain to be imported for free, rather than placing a high tax on it as was the custom.

ENGLAND

Did you ever wonder who invented the sandwich? It was created by John Montague, the English Earl of Sandwich. His title became the name for that food you carry to school in your lunch box!

The story is that he once played cards at a men's club in London for twenty-four hours straight. He didn't want to risk his luck by leaving the table to eat, so he asked that his meat be brought to him between two slices of bread so that he could hold his food in one hand and his cards in the other.

That was the first sandwich.

AMERICA

In 1785, American inventor Oliver Evans created the first automatic flour mill. This was a heavy roller that ran over the grains and ground them. Today, the steel wheel that came from Mr. Evans's invention is still used for much of the mass production of grain.

Around this time, the Colonists were becoming quite adept at making different kinds of breads. Hoecakes were popular little rolls in Colonial times. They were made by setting small round breads on iron hoes, which were then held over the fire to bake, much in the same way you might roast marshmallows over a campfire.

Johnnycakes were pancakes made from oatmeal and water. They were grilled over the fire indoors and served at nearly every meal. No one knows exactly where the term *Johnnycake* comes from, but it could come from "journey cake"—for breads that the Pilgrims took on long journeys across the sea.

Many of the breads invented during this time in American history are still popular today, including Johnnycakes and Third Bread.

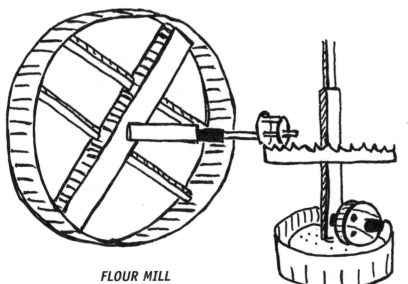

FLOUR MILL

Johnnycakes

You can make these traditional Johnnycakes and serve them any time of the day, just like the Colonists did.

HERE'S WHAT YOU'LL NEED:

1 cup water

2 tablespoons butter, plus extra for oiling the pan

1 cup cornmeal

½ teaspoon salt

½ teaspoon sugar

½ cup milk

HERE'S WHAT YOU'LL DO:

1. Bring the water and 2 tablespoons butter to a boil in a saucepan over medium-high heat.
2. Mix the cornmeal, salt, and sugar in a bowl and pour the water and butter mixture in. Add the milk and stir.
3. Put a skillet on the stove over medium heat and melt some more butter on it, tipping the pan to get the butter all over it.
4. Spoon the batter in pancake-sized dollops onto the hot skillet. Cook for 5 minutes on each side or until golden brown.
5. Serve hot, topped with jam, syrup, or apple butter.

Makes 12 Johnnycakes

Colonial Third Bread

This is called Third Bread because it uses three main ingredients: two flours and one meal.

HERE'S WHAT YOU'LL NEED:

2 teaspoons (³⁄₄ package) yeast

1½ cups bread flour

½ cup rye flour

½ cup cornmeal

⅓ cup honey

1 teaspoon salt

1 cup water

Extra butter, for greasing

HERE'S WHAT YOU'LL DO:

1. Mix all the ingredients in a large bowl with your hands to make a smooth, elastic dough.
2. Turn the dough out onto a floured counter and knead for 10 minutes.
3. Return the dough to a bowl and cover it with a dish towel. Leave it to rise for 1 hour, then punch it down and let it rest for 15 minutes.
4. Heat the oven to 350°F and grease a loaf pan with butter. Put the dough in the pan and let it rise for 30 minutes.
5. Bake the bread for 50 minutes. Make sure it's browned on top and sounds hollow when you knock on it. If it isn't ready, heat it 5 minutes at a time until it is.
6. Serve Third Bread warm or cold.

Makes 1 loaf

FRANCE

Marie Antoinette was the queen of France. Her husband was King Louis XVI. They reigned just before the French Revolution, and the people hated them because they led frivolous lives and spent money extravagantly even though the rest of the country was very poor. People were starving because they couldn't afford to eat; they couldn't even buy bread.

When Marie Antoinette was told that the peasants were angry because they had no bread to eat, she was so unaware of how the poor were living that she thought it meant they had simply run out of bread, but that they had meat, vegetables, fruit, wines, and everything else the queen enjoyed in her own life.

With that in mind, when she was told, "They have no bread" she responded with the famous comment, "Let them eat cake."

Anger over bread isn't a thing of the past. In 1996, people living in Jordan in the Middle East rioted when the government doubled the price of bread. The people burned banks and other government buildings and fought with police. Lots of people were hurt, and more than 150 people were arrested.

ENGLAND

England was not a good place for orphans in the 1800s. Charles Dickens wrote many stories about children who had to try to make it on their own on the rough streets of London. One of the best-known of these stories is *Oliver Twist*, which is about a poor orphan who had to pick pockets for a living. The sad part is that while Dickens might not have known a boy named Oliver Twist, there were probably hundreds of boys and girls like him back then.

There is a rich, tasty egg bread called Sally Lunn that's as popular today as it was in Dickens's time. The story goes that there was a young girl in nineteenth-century England named Sally Lunn. She was an orphan who had no one to take care of her, so at an early age she had to start making her own money. She did this by making tasty breads and selling them on the street corners in London.

She must have done a good job of it because we're still making and eating Sally Lunn bread today, and nearly every bread cookbook has a different version of it.

Sally Lunn Bread

HERE'S WHAT YOU'LL NEED:

2 teaspoons (¾ package) yeast

2 cups bread flour or all-purpose flour

1 tablespoon sugar

1 teaspoon salt

4 tablespoons (½ stick) butter, plus extra for greasing

2 eggs

¾ cup water or milk

HERE'S WHAT YOU'LL DO:

1. Mix all the ingredients well in a large mixing bowl or the bowl of an electric mixer.
2. Turn the dough out onto a lightly floured counter and knead for 10 minutes. The dough should be smooth and elastic.
3. Put the dough into a greased bowl. Cover with a dish towel and let it sit in a warm place until the dough has doubled in bulk. This should take about 1½ hours.
4. Punch the dough down and let it rest for 5 minutes while you grease a loaf pan.
5. Put the dough into the greased pan, cover it with a cloth, and let it sit in a warm place for 30 minutes or until it's doubled in bulk again. Heat the oven to 350°F.
6. Bake the bread for 35–40 minutes. You'll know it's done when you knock on the top and it sounds hollow.

Makes 1 loaf

Another street corner bread comes from Latin America. *Bunuelos* are pastries that are deep-fried to make them very crispy. They're topped with cinnamon and sugar. Even today you can often find them sold on the street as snacks.

This is such a tasty treat that other countries make almost the same thing but call it by a different name. In France, it's called *galettes a l'huile*, and in Italy *farfallette dolci*.

ENGLAND

Beginning in 1837, the English farmers suffered year after year of bad harvests. The grain supplies became lower and lower until finally, in the middle of the 1840s, there was no grain left at all. This lack of grain was called a famine. The people couldn't buy grain from other countries because the tax was too high. The price of bread became very high and the poorer people starved.

Welsh Rabbit

No, there's no actual rabbit in this dish! It's called that because the poor Welsh peasants who couldn't afford meat made this cheese and bread dish for Sunday dinner.

It's a far better treat than real rabbit, I'd say.

Non-alcoholic beer is available in most grocery stores, but you can use chicken broth instead if you prefer.

Always have an adult's help when using the stove and oven broiler.

HERE'S WHAT YOU'LL NEED:

4 tablespoons (1/2 stick) butter

1/4 cup flour

1/2 teaspoon dry mustard

1/2 teaspoon Worcestershire sauce

3/4 cup milk

3/4 cup beer

2 cups shredded cheddar cheese

8 slices whole wheat toast

HERE'S WHAT YOU'LL DO:

1. Melt the butter in a 2-quart saucepan over low heat. Stir in the flour, mustard, and Worcestershire sauce.
2. Stir constantly until smooth and bubbly, then remove the pan from the heat. Stir in the milk and beer and heat to boiling, stirring constantly. Add the cheese and warm until melted.
3. Arrange the toast slices on an ungreased cookie sheet. Spoon about 1/3 cup sauce onto each slice. Set the oven control to broil or 550°F.
4. Broil 3 minutes or until cheese is light brown.

Makes 8 servings

AMERICA

Though the Civil War made the 1860s a nightmare for American history, the middle 1800s were an interesting time in the development of food. This is partly because it was around this time that stoves came into use. Not everyone had a stove, though, and many people cooked the old-fashioned way in the fire. Cookbooks from the 1800s often have instructions for both fire cooking and stove cooking.

Many of the dishes that we still enjoy today have roots in this time period. One of the main foods that comes to mind is hush puppies, which were invented in the 1860s. According to some sources, cooks made little pieces of fried bread to give to dogs so they would stop barking. For example, hush puppies could be taken along on a fishing trip, so the dogs wouldn't bark and scare the fish away.

It's hard to bark with your mouth full!

Another theory of how hush puppies were created is that the enslaved people of the Antebellum time (before the Civil War and freedom) were allowed only six quarts of cornmeal and three pounds of bacon to eat every week. Clever cooks combined the bacon fat and cornmeal to make what we think of today as hush puppies.

Regardless of which story is true, hush puppies are most definitely a Southern dish. Some of the finest Southern restaurants are proud to have them on the menu, even alongside more sophisticated dishes like lobster and prime rib.

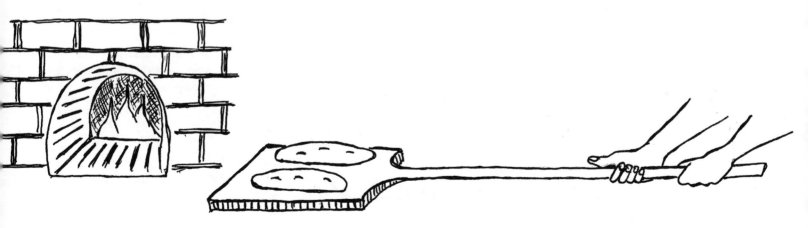

Hush Puppies

HERE'S WHAT YOU'LL NEED:

1½ cups cornmeal

½ cup flour

2 teaspoons baking powder

½ teaspoon salt

1 egg

1 small onion, peeled and chopped

¾ cup milk

1¼ pounds (5 sticks) butter

HERE'S WHAT YOU'LL DO:

1. Mix the cornmeal, flour, baking powder, and salt in a bowl.
2. In a second bowl, beat the egg lightly, then add the onion and milk. Stir.
3. Add the onion, milk, and egg mixture to the flour mixture and stir well.
4. Heat a frying pan or skillet over medium-high heat and melt the butter. It will be very hot, so be very careful and have an adult's help when working with it.
5. Drop the hush puppy batter onto the hot buttered skillet one spoonful at a time and fry on each side for a couple of minutes until browned.
6. Remove the cooked hush puppies from the hot butter and drain them on paper towels.
7. Eat them up!

Makes 18 hush puppies

QUICK BREADS

Around the time of the Civil War, quick breads became popular. Women who used to be at home all day to tend a rising loaf were suddenly given many new duties away from home, like working as nurses in the makeshift hospitals set up to help soldiers injured in the war. They needed bread that would be ready in a hurry.

Quick breads are called quick breads because they don't require yeast and therefore they don't require all of the time spent on kneading, rising, and resting.

But what makes the bread rise if there's no yeast? There are other leaveners, such as baking soda and baking powder. Baking soda comes in a box, and people usually buy large boxes. Baking powder almost always comes in a tin that's shaped like a soup can, only smaller. Because of this, people tend to think that baking powder is stronger than baking soda, but that's not true. Baking powder is a mixture of baking soda and another leavener, cream of tartar.

Because baking powder has the additional leavener, cream of tartar, in it, it's called "double acting." That simply means that there are two active ingredients rather than one.

To make things even more confusing, many recipes call for both baking soda and baking powder. You might ask why, and that's a good question. The answer is that different breads need different strengths of leavener to make it rise (because of denser ingredients, for example). Using both increases rising power.

Cranberry Quick Bread

HERE'S WHAT YOU'LL NEED:

3 cups all-purpose flour

1 teaspoon baking soda

1 teaspoon baking powder

1 teaspoon salt

1¼ cups milk

2 eggs

1 cup sugar

4 tablespoons (½ stick) butter, melted and cooled, plus extra for greasing

1 cup raw cranberries, chopped

¾ cup walnut pieces (optional)

If you want to see baking soda and baking powder at work, here's how to make a quick bread like the ones that would have been made in the 1800s. Thanksgiving is a great time to make this great American favorite.

HERE'S WHAT YOU'LL DO:

1. Mix the flour, baking soda, baking powder, salt, and milk in one bowl.
2. Stir the eggs and sugar together in another bowl and add the melted butter slowly.
3. Add egg and sugar mixture to the milk and flour mixture. You should have a smooth batter.
4. Mix the cranberries and walnuts in very carefully so you don't break them up too much.
5. Heat the oven to 350°F and grease a loaf pan.
6. Put the bread mixture into the loaf pan and bake for 1 hour. Don't worry if the top of the bread breaks. This tends to happen with quick breads.
7. If you can resist eating it right away, wrap the loaf in aluminum foil and let it sit overnight before eating it. Some people swear this is the way to bring out the best taste in the bread.

Makes 1 loaf

BEYOND BAKING

Baking soda is as interesting as yeast. In fact, it's a lot like yeast in that it's a bread leavener, or something that pumps out gas bubbles and makes the bread puff.

Because of this very thing, there are other things you can do with baking soda besides baking. You can use baking soda as a refrigerator deodorizer (baking soda absorbs wetness and odor, so if you put an open box in the fridge it won't smell bad), as a kitchen cleaner, and as a bathroom cleaner. There are even some toothpastes that contain baking soda! You can also use baking soda as a hand cleaner—if you get sticky stuff on your hands and it won't come off with water (like resin from your Christmas tree), rub a little baking soda in and then rinse it off. The sticky stuff will be gone.

In fact, many of the ingredients in bread can be used for more than just baking. Here's three different ways.

In 1846 the first commercial baking soda was created in New York City by Austin Church and John Dwight.

Poster Paints

HERE'S WHAT YOU'LL NEED:

1/4 cup flour

1 cup water

6 tablespoons water

3 lidded jars (like baby food jars)

3 colors food coloring

1 teaspoon dish detergent (optional)

HERE'S WHAT YOU'LL DO:

1. Mix the flour and water in a small saucepan to make a thick paste and heat it over medium heat for 2–4 minutes.
2. When the mixture starts to get very thick, remove it from the heat.
3. Put 2 tablespoons water into each jar, then add one-third of the flour paste and enough food coloring to make the color you want.
4. To make a shinier finish, add 4 drops of liquid dish detergent to each jar and mix well.
5. Paint! You can use these paints just like any other poster paints. Though this paint is made from flour, it isn't for eating or putting on food—it tastes terrible!

Makes 9 ounces

Squeeze Paints

HERE'S WHAT YOU'LL NEED:

1 cup flour

¼ cup salt

¼ cup sugar

¾ cup water

4 plastic squeeze bottles (old mustard bottles are perfect)

4 colors food coloring

Glitter (optional)

HERE'S WHAT YOU'LL DO:

1. Mix the flour, salt, sugar, and water in a bowl and put one-fourth of the mixture in each of the four bottles.
2. Put a few drops of 1 color food coloring into each bottle, then screw the lids on tightly.
3. Shake the bottles to mix the color in. Check to see if it's the right shade. If it's too light, add two drops of food coloring at a time until you have the right color.
4. Squeeze the paints onto thick paper and make designs. This paint dries in thick lumps, like puff paint. If you like, you can add sparkles to your design before the paint dries.
5. Like the poster paint, this paint isn't good for eating. You'll have more fun putting it on paper than on your food or in your mouth.

Makes 8 ounces

Play Dough

HERE'S WHAT YOU'LL NEED:

1½ cups flour

½ cup salt

½ cup water

¼ cup oil

½ teaspoon vanilla extract (optional)

Food coloring (optional)

Airtight containers for storage

HERE'S WHAT YOU'LL DO:

1. Put the flour and salt in a bowl and slowly add the water and oil, mixing with your hands. If the mixture is too crumbly to form into shapes, add a little more water. If it's too sticky, add more flour.
2. If you want the dough to smell sweet, add the vanilla extract. Though the dough won't hurt you if you eat it, don't add the vanilla to dough that young children will using because they might think it's candy. The dough is not harmful if it's accidentally eaten, but it certainly does not taste good.
3. Divide the dough into sections and work a few drops of food coloring into each until the color is smooth and even.
4. The play dough will keep for 2–4 weeks stored in airtight containers.

Makes 16 ounces

AMERICA

It was around 1925 that stores began selling bread already sliced. Before that everyone bought their bread in whole loaves and took it home to slice.

Many people found this to be a wonderful convenience, and that's why today there is the expression "the greatest thing since sliced bread."

SCOTLAND

Before 1928, people died of diseases that just keep you out of school for a couple of days now. That's because they didn't have the antibiotic drugs we have today to fight bacterial illness.

But in 1928, Sir Alexander Fleming, a Scottish physician and bacteriologist, discovered a mold from the family of *Penicillium notatum* in bread. He called it "penicillin" and found it could be used to save people from all kinds of deadly diseases. Some of the things that penicillin cures are pneumonia, meningitis, tonsillitis, scarlet fever, boils, and strep throat.

In honor of his very important discovery, Sir Alexander Fleming was one of three winners of the Nobel prize for medicine in 1945.

Grow Mold

This is the same sort of bread mold that Sir Fleming first found. It's easiest to see the mold on white bread, but it also takes longer to grow there.

HERE'S WHAT YOU'LL NEED:

1 paper towel

1 cake pan

1 slice bread

2 feet plastic wrap

HERE'S WHAT YOU'LL DO:

1. Dampen the paper towel and lay it in the cake pan.
2. Put the slice of bread on top of the damp paper towel.
3. Cover the pan with plastic wrap and secure the edges so air doesn't get in.
4. Put the cake pan in a dark, cool place. A pantry under the sink is perfect.
5. Let the bread sit undisturbed for 3 days, then look at it. Clusters of mold will be visible to the eye!

DON'T EAT THIS—YUCK!

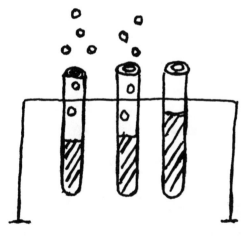

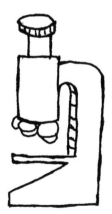

AMERICA

Nineteen thirty-two was the year of the Great Depression in America. The stock market crashed and everyone lost their money. Even people who had their money safely tucked away in banks lost everything, because the banks lost everything. It's hard to imagine, but some people who were millionaires one day were selling flowers for pennies apiece on street corners the next.

In every city and town in America, huge numbers of people were hungry. Many of them waited in charity bread lines for hours, hoping to get something to eat. Loaves of bread cost five cents each but even so were too expensive for many people to buy.

A LOOK INSIDE A MODERN BAKERY

In the old days, bakeries were the only place for people to get bread, so there was at least one in every village and people went every day. Today there are still lots of bakeries, even though big grocery stores sell bread along with everything else.

Jack Corkey is a baker, and so is his wife, Laurie. Together they own and run the Great Harvest Bakery in Herndon, Virginia. Mr. Corkey says that people begin the daily bread baking in his shop each day at 4:30 A.M., and continue to bake until noon.

The first thing the bakers do is grind grain, which they have shipped from Montana, into flour with an electric-powered stone mill. That grain is then allowed to cool for a day, and the bakers take out the flour that they made the previous day for the second step.

Then they put all of the bread ingredients, like flour, fresh yeast, butter, milk, and whatever flavorings, fruits, or nuts they might be using into a big, barrel-shaped bowl. The bowl is about three and one-half feet tall and two and one-half feet wide, to accommodate lots of bread dough. The ingredients are put in by

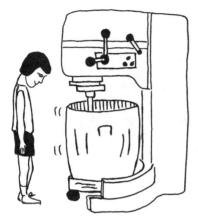

people, not by a machine. The bakers put this huge bowl under an electric mixer that has a big dough hook, and the dough is mixed and kneaded by the machine.

When the ingredients are mixed and smooth, the bakers take the dough out and do some more kneading by hand. Then they shape the loaves and put them into an enormous oven. The professional baker's oven has shelves that revolve like a Ferris wheel, and in Mr. and Mrs. Corkey's oven, each shelf holds about seventy loaves. The bread is baked, cooled, and put into plastic bags for the day's customers.

The bakers make about six different kinds of bread this way each day. Some bakeries, though, make only white bread, and that's what's most common in groceries.

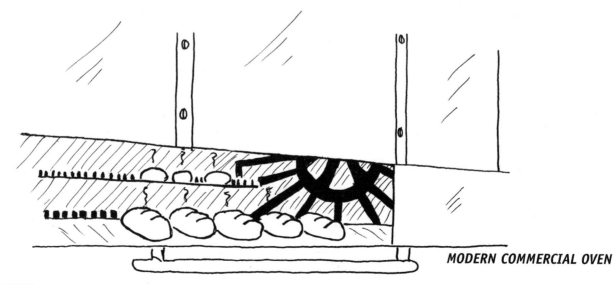

MODERN COMMERCIAL OVEN

White Bread

This is about the easiest yeast bread you can make, and it's also the most versatile. You can do anything with it.

HERE'S WHAT YOU'LL NEED:

2 teaspoons (¾ package) yeast

2 cups bread flour or all-purpose flour

2 teaspoons sugar

½ teaspoon salt

2 tablespoons butter, plus extra for greasing

¾ cup water or milk

HERE'S WHAT YOU'LL DO:

1. Combine all the ingredients in a large bowl and mix well.
2. Shake a little flour onto a clean counter top and put the bread dough on it. Knead the dough, pulling, stretching, and folding, for 10 minutes. It should be smooth and elastic.
3. Grease a bowl and put the bread dough into it. Cover it with a dish towel and let it sit in a warm place until the dough has doubled in bulk. This should take about 1½ hours.
4. Punch the dough down and let it rest for 5 minutes while you grease a loaf pan.
5. Put the dough into the greased pan, cover it with a dish cloth, and let it sit in a warm place for 30 minutes or until it's doubled in bulk again. Heat the oven to 350°F.
6. Bake for 35–40 minutes. You'll know it's done when you knock on the top and it sounds hollow.

Makes 1 loaf

esides white bread, bakers all over the world make hundreds of types of bread every day. But where do the bakers get all the ideas for those different kinds of bread? A lot of them are traditional recipes, like nine grain, white bread, and whole wheat bread. But many bakers also experiment with different kinds of flavors to see what tastes good together.

They share ideas, too. If a baker comes up with a really tasty bread that lots of people like—such as the honey wheat bread at Mr. and Mrs. Corkey's store—they'll share the recipe with other bakers.

But certain breads have set recipes that never change.

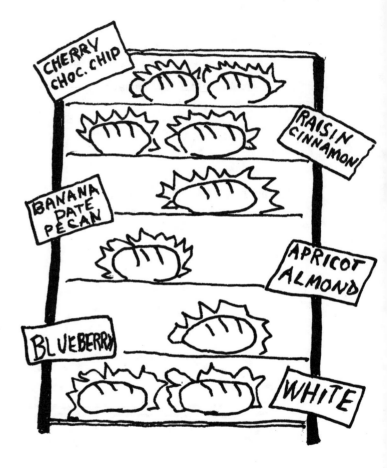

French Baguette Pans

In France, the government actually tells bakers what they can put into the famous French bread—if it has anything other than water, flour, yeast, and salt in it, it's not French bread.

The loaves, called *baguettes*, are long and slender, like big pencils. They're baked in special pans that sell in some stores for lots of money, but you can make your own baguette pans at home.

HERE'S WHAT YOU'LL NEED:

8 feet aluminum foil

HERE'S WHAT YOU'LL DO:

1. Fold the aluminum foil over three times so you have a very thick piece of 2-foot aluminum foil.
2. Fold the foil in half lengthwise.
3. Gently shape the long sides into "U" shapes. You should now have a 2-foot-long pan that looks like a "W" from the sides.

Makes 1 baguette pan that holds two loaves

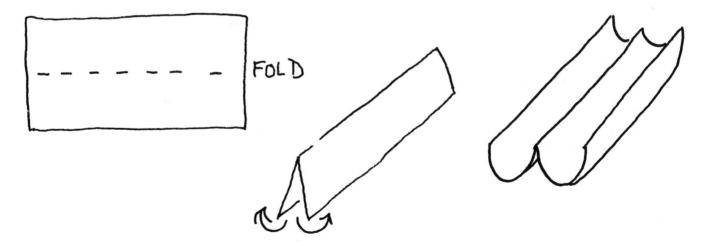

ALUMINUM FOIL

FOLD

French Bread

This is really great bread because you can use it for everything! It's particularly good dipped in melted cheese (fondue) or for cheese sandwiches. Genuine French bread doesn't contain butter, but adding just a little helps it stay fresh longer and taste better.

HERE'S WHAT YOU'LL NEED:

4 teaspoons (1¼ packages) yeast

4 cups white flour

2 tablespoons butter, plus extra for greasing

1½ cups water

HERE'S WHAT YOU'LL NEED:

1. Combine all of the ingredients in a large bowl and mix so that all the dry ingredients are dampened.
2. Put the dough on a floured table and knead it for 10 minutes, folding it over and stretching it out and back. You should end up with a smooth loaf that doesn't stick to your fingers but is easy to shape. If you need to add more flour or water, add just a teaspoon at a time until you have the right consistency.
3. Put the dough into a greased bowl and let it sit in a warm place for 1 hour or until the dough has doubled in bulk.
4. Punch the dough down and let it rest for 15 minutes.
5. Divide the dough into two pieces and roll them out with your hands the

way you would if you were making snakes out of play dough. When the dough snakes are almost as long as your baguette pan, put them into each side of it and cover them with a dry dish towel.

6. Let the dough baguettes rise for 30 minutes. Heat the oven to 400°F.
7. Bake 30 minutes. They're done when they're golden brown and sound hollow when you knock on them.

Makes 2 (deux!) baguettes

WELCOME TO MODERN BAKERY

HONEY WHOLE WHEAT $3.00
NINE GRAIN $3.30
ONION DILL $3.75
SUNFLOWER $3.45
RAISIN CINNAMON $3.45

At the end of the day in a modern bakery, all the bread that hasn't been sold is used for making other things. Some bakers make their own croutons out of stale bread and package them for sale. Others give the bread to the poor, since it's still tasty and nutritious even after it's been sitting on the shelf all day. Still others feed ducks with it.

There are lots of things to do with stale bread; here are two ideas.

Croutons

You can make crunchy, tasty croutons for salads or soups using almost any flavorings that you like.

HERE'S WHAT YOU'LL NEED:

2 tablespoons butter

2 tablespoons olive oil

1 clove garlic, minced

2 cups stale bread cubes

Salt and pepper, to taste

2 tablespoons grated parmesan cheese

HERE'S WHAT YOU'LL DO:

1. Heat the butter and olive oil in a frying pan over medium-high heat until it's melted but not burned.
2. Add the garlic and stir it around in the oil and butter mixture.
3. Fry the bread cubes until they're crisp, and then put them on a plate and sprinkle with salt, pepper, and parmesan cheese.
4. The croutons are ready to serve as soon as they've cooled!

Makes 2 cups

French Toast

You've probably had French toast before, but did you know the history behind it? This is a very old dish, traditionally made by European peasants in order to use every last bit of their bread, even once it was stale.

To make really authentic French toast, make the egg mixture and soak the bread in it overnight in the refrigerator. If you don't want to wait, you can make it all at the same time.

Top your French toast with either powdered confectioners' sugar or maple syrup.

HERE'S WHAT YOU'LL NEED:

2 eggs

¼ cup milk or cream

2 teaspoons sugar

Pinch of salt

¼ teaspoon ground cinnamon

½ teaspoon vanilla extract (optional)

4 thick slices stale bread

Extra butter, for greasing (optional)

Powdered sugar or maple syrup, to taste

HERE'S WHAT YOU'LL DO:

1. Whisk the eggs, milk or cream, sugar, salt, cinnamon, and vanilla extract in a shallow bowl.
2. Soak the slices of stale bread in the egg mixture for 10 minutes or overnight in the refrigerator.

3. Heat a large frying pan over medium-high heat, and brown the bread slices on each side. If you like, you can add a little butter to the pan to keep the toast from sticking.
4. Serve hot with powdered sugar or syrup.

Makes 4 servings

The real name of French toast is, in French, *pain perdu*. That means "lost bread," and it's called that because French bread grows stale so quickly that if you leave it out for just one night it's too hard to eat in the morning.

So the French had to be resourceful and think of a way to use it so it wouldn't be "lost bread." Soaking the stale bread in milk and egg softened it up, but made it too mushy. They had to cook it to make it easy to eat.

And that's why we have French toast today.

BREAD AROUND THE WORLD

Today bread is tremendously important to people in nearly every culture. And every culture seems to have its own special bread that stands out as distinctly as a flag:

America: Corn bread
France: Baguette (French bread), Croissant
Italy: Panettone
England: Scones, Crumpets
Latin America: Bunuelos
Sweden: Rye crisp
Russia: Pumpernickel
Middle East: Pita bread
India: Chapatis, Pappadam
Mexico: Corn tortilla
Israel: Challah

Italy: Panettone

France: Baguette, Croissant

England: Crumpets

Israel: Challah

Mexico: Corn tortilla

Did you know that English muffins aren't actually English at all? They're an American invention but are called English muffins because they look like traditional English crumpets. Crumpets are round, fried cakes made from baking soda batter. They have little holes in the top of them where heat bubbles have popped and are served with jam and butter.

HOLIDAY BREADS

Just as every culture in the world has its own special bread, each seems to have a special bread or two for their national holidays. Many traditional American and European Christmas breads have cinnamon and ginger and other spices, as well as candied fruits. Greek holiday breads have lots of dill and often yogurt and egg. Scandinavian breads are heavy, made from rye, and perfect for making sandwiches with meat and mustard.

Some cultures, like Mexican, bake trinkets into holiday bread so that the person who finds the trinket in his or her piece of bread will have good luck.

Making these breads and eating them is a great way to learn about other cultures.

In England it was believed that on Halloween night the souls of the dead could once again walk the earth. A strange custom grew out of that belief: men and women used to go out "a-souling," which meant that they would go from house to house saying:

A soul cake, a soul cake,

A penny or a soul cake!

The people in the houses would give them either pennies or little pastries called soul cakes. In exchange the men and women were to say a prayer for the dead.

HERE'S WHAT YOU'LL NEED:

2 teaspoons (¾ package) yeast

Bread

2½ cups bread flour

½ cup sugar

½ teaspoon salt

8 tablespoons (1 stick) butter, melted, plus extra for greasing

3 eggs, beaten

¼ cup water

½ cup milk

1 teaspoon of grated lemon rind

¼ cup raisins

¼ cup pecan nuts

1 dry pinto bean

Icing

¼ cup confectioners' sugar

½ teaspoon lemon juice

½ teaspoon water or enough to make a thick paste

Rosco de Reyes (Mexican New Year's Bread)

This is a traditional Mexican holiday bread, which is baked in the shaped of a ring and served for good luck on New Year's Day.

Put a pinto bean in the bread, and the person who gets the bean in his or her piece will have good luck in the coming year.

HERE'S WHAT YOU'LL DO:

1. To make the bread, combine all the ingredients except for the icing ingredients in a large bowl and knead with your hands for 10 minutes until you have a smooth, elastic dough. Return the dough to the bowl.
2. Cover the bowl with a dish towel and set it in a warm place for 1 hour so the dough can rise.
3. After the dough has risen, punch it down and then let it rest for 15 minutes.
4. Shape the dough into a ring on a greased cookie sheet and let it rise for 30 minutes more. Heat the oven to 350°F.
5. Bake for 40 minutes. Make sure the ring is lightly browned and sounds hollow when you knock on it. If it's still too light and doughy, bake 5 minutes more.
6. Take the bread out of the oven. To make the icing, mix the sugar, lemon juice, and water while the bread cools.
7. When the bread has cooled, spread the icing paste on it and serve. Remember that the person who gets the slice with the pinto bean will have good luck!

Makes 1 loaf

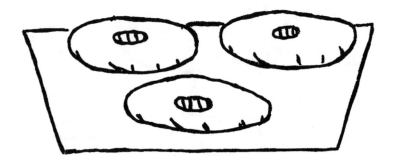

Did you know that those tasty corn chips you use for salsa, chili, and cheese dip are made from Mexican corn tortillas? In Mexico, the tortilla is an important part of the diet—it's the main bread they eat. Tortillas are made from cornmeal and water, and they're baked on a hot griddle until crispy. Not only are they good this way but you can wrap them around almost anything to make a Mexican-style sandwich.

Moravian Christmas Bread

This is an interesting traditional European Christmas bread. It takes a long time to make, but the results are worth it. It's delicious either plain or spread with cinnamon, sugar, and butter.

HERE'S WHAT YOU'LL NEED:

Bread

1 cup milk

⅓ cup currants

2 teaspoons (¾ package) yeast

2½ cups flour

¼ cup sugar

½ teaspoon salt

5½ tablespoons (almost ¾ stick) butter, melted, plus extra for greasing

3 tablespoons chopped candied pineapple

3 tablespoons chopped candied lemon rind

3 tablespoons chopped candied orange rind

Glaze

1 egg

1 tablespoon water

HERE'S WHAT YOU'LL DO:

1. To make the bread, in a small pot, scald the milk. This means to heat it over low heat until almost boiling. You'll know it's ready when small bubbles start to form around the edge of the liquid. When it's ready, take it off the heat and let it cool to lukewarm.

2. In a separate pot, scald the currants. To do this, gently heat the currants and 1 cup water until nearly boiling. Then remove the pot, drain the currants, and set them on a paper towel to dry.

3. Mix the milk, currants, yeast, flour, sugar, salt, 5½ tablespoons melted butter, candied pineapple, and candied rinds in a large bowl with your hands to make a smooth, elastic dough.

4. Turn the dough out onto a floured counter and knead for at least 10 minutes.

5. Return the dough to a bowl and cover it with a dish towel. Leave it to rise for 1 hour, then punch it down and let it rest for 15 minutes.

6. Heat the oven to 350°F and grease a loaf pan. Put the dough in the pan and let it rise for 30 minutes.

7. Bake for 50 minutes. Make sure it's browned on top and sounds hol-low when you knock on it. If it isn't ready, bake it 5 minutes at a time until it is.

8. While the bread bakes, make the glaze. Beat the egg and 1 tablespoon water together. This glaze will give the loaf a gourmet-looking shine.

9. When the bread is done, turn off the oven and paint the glaze on top of the loaf with a pastry brush. Return the loaf to the still-warm oven for 5 minutes to set the glaze.

10. Enjoy your bread!

Makes 1 loaf

Have an International Breakfast

Now that you've learned about breads around the world, you can share an international breakfast with your class or a group of your friends. You can make the bread of a foreign country and learn how to call the foods by their foreign names. For example, you might choose to have a French breakfast:

Bread	*pain*	(PAN)
Butter	*bêurre*	(BURR)
Milk	*lait*	(LAY)
Eggs	*oeufs*	(UFFS)
"Enjoy your meal!"	*Bon appetit!*	(bon a-pa-TEE)

GLOSSARY

Ale is a type of hearty beer that has been brewed for centuries. It contains yeast and was probably added to bread dough to make the first yeast bread.

All-purpose flour is made from hard wheat or a blend of high-gluten hard wheat and low-gluten soft wheat. Hard wheat is best for making bread because it causes loaves to be light and fluffy. All-purpose flour is made from the central part of the grain, and so it doesn't have any wheat germ or bran, which are two of the more nutritious parts. It is available bleached and unbleached. Bleaching makes flour whiter and helps pastries and cakes rise. If you go to the grocery store and look in the bulk foods section you'll see that except for the colors, bleached and unbleached flours don't look very different from each other. Bleaching is usually done with chemicals and though these chemicals don't stay in the flour, it's best to buy unbleached flour if you're making something other than cakes or pastries.

Archaeologists are people who study ancient civilizations to learn how they lived. One of the most important things they look for is evidence of what the ancient people ate. One of the most common finds is evidence of bread in the form of grains, grain mills, and other tools relating to the mixing of breads. Thanks to archaeologists we know about the role bread played in ancient civilizations like the prehistoric Asians, Mesopotamians, Greeks, and Romans.

Bakers bake food. Bakers don't only bake bread; they also make cakes, cookies, muffins, rolls, pastries, and anything else that gets mixed up into a dough or batter and baked in the oven. The first professional bakers were in ancient Rome, 2,300 years ago.

A **bakery** is a store that sells baked foods. It has ovens, huge mixers, bowls, and refrigerators, along with plenty of workers to put it all together. Most bakeries specialize in breads, pastries, cookies, or bagels. The first bakeries, like the first bakers, were started in ancient Rome 2,300 years ago.

Barley flour is made from barley and is low in gluten, which is what makes loaves fluffy. Barley flour must be used with either pure gluten, which you can sometimes buy at the store, or with a flour that's naturally high in gluten, like whole wheat flour.

Bread is crushed grain mixed with a "binding agent" (something wet that makes it hold together, like water, milk, or eggs) and then baked.

Bread flour is a blend of 99.8 percent hard wheat flour and small amounts of malted barley flour to enhance the yeast activity. This is the best flour for making light, fluffy loaves.

But, like all-purpose flour, it doesn't contain the wheat germ or the bran.

A **bread machine** is an appliance for people to use in their own kitchens to make bread. It has a bucket with an electronic arm at the bottom of it to knead the bread. It heats up and bakes the bread as well, so the baker has only to combine the ingredients in the bucket, and then take the loaf out at the end.

Butter is a "shortening" or a "fat" that helps make bread tender. It also makes it taste delicious. Butter is tasty both in and on bread.

Eggs are important in bread because they help make the bread even fluffier than it would be with just the leavener. They also add taste, a pretty golden color, and good nutrition.

Enriched flour is flour that has lost most of its fiber and nutrients in the milling process. The miller then adds iron, thiamine, riboflavin, niacin, and other vitamins and minerals.

Gluten is the high-protein flour (also called "hard" flour) that is left when the starch is rinsed from whole wheat flour. It holds the gas bubbles released by the yeast in the bread, so the bread gets tall and fluffy. Kneading stretches out the gluten, making it easier for the gluten to hold in the gas bubbles. Gluten is very important if you want a high loaf of bread. The most high-gluten flour is bread flour.

Kneading is the process of pulling bread dough apart and folding it back onto itself. The purpose of this is to stretch the protein gluten so that the bread will be able to rise properly. This is not unlike stretching a balloon before you try to blow it up.

Leavened bread is bread that is light and fluffy. It contains a **leavener**, which is the thing that makes bread dough rise. The most common leaveners are yeast, baking soda, baking powder (which is a mixture of baking soda and cream of tartar), or a sponge.

Milk makes bread soft and tender to chew. It also adds nutrition. Not all bread recipes call for milk. Some call for water alone. Some bread recipes call for water and dry milk powder, which is basically milk.

Milling is to crush grain to separate the three parts of seed: the germ, the endosperm, and the bran. The endosperm is the part that's usually crushed into flour, although the germ and the bran have lots of nutrition and fiber. The first milling was done by crushing grain between two flat rocks. Later, mills were powered by animals, who pulled the heavy stones the grind the grain in between. These were first invented around 700 B.C.

Oats are a very nutritious addition to bread, since they have lots of protein and vitamins. Oatmeal bread was a favorite among early American settlers.

Salt slows the action of the yeast so the bread dough doesn't get too high and then collapse before you're able to bake it.

Self-rising flour is all-purpose flour with added baking soda and salt, so the leavener is built in. In the 1940s people thought this was a great flour because they didn't have to buy the soda and salt separately, but today self-rising flour is used for very little.

Shortening is a common term for the ingredient that makes bread tender, usually butter. Most recipes don't call for "shortening" anymore. In the old days, people couldn't always go to the grocery store and buy butter. Sometimes it wasn't available at all, and other times (like during World War II) they could only buy small amounts of it with special coupons. So when a recipe called for shortening, the cook knew that he or she could use whatever was on hand: butter, oil, lard, bacon fat, or margarine. Today, most recipes call for what will taste best in the bread. Usually it's butter or margarine, but the clever cook who has run out of butter or whatever the recipe calls for can substitute it with whatever is on hand.

A **sponge** is a leavener, which means it makes bread dough rise. It's a thick batter of flour and milk or water that sits out in a bowl. Usually this bowl of sponge is left uncovered so that the yeast spores that float around in the air can get into it and multiply. Once the sponge is filled with yeast spores it gets bubbly and can be used in place of packaged yeast. A sponge must be used every week to keep it fresh. This is done by removing one cup of it and adding more flour and milk or water.

Starch is made by plants and animals as a way of storing sugars. A starch molecule is made of long chains of sugar molecules. It can easily be changed back to sugar when needed. Like sugar, starches also absorb water. When starches are heated with water, they swell and increase in size. This property makes them very useful as thickeners for sauces and gravies.

Sugar feeds the yeast and makes it produce the carbon dioxide necessary to make a fluffy loaf of bread. If you don't have sugar you can use anything that's naturally sweet, including brown sugar, molasses, honey, barley malt, or corn syrup.

Water gives the bread a nice brown crust and may be used in place of milk in most recipes.

Whole wheat flour has a stronger flavor than bread flour, and it contains wheat germ, which makes it higher in fiber and nutrition. It also has more fat and therefore has to be kept in the refrigerator so that it doesn't spoil.

Yeast are one-celled plants that are distant cousins of mushrooms. Like mushrooms and other plants that do not contain chlorophyll, yeast plants cannot make their own food and must get it from their surroundings. Yeast does this by "eating" sugars. When a yeast spore eats a sweetener, it lets out gas bubbles made of carbon monoxide. When yeast is in bread, these bubbles are trapped by the other ingredients (especially the gluten in flour), making the bread tall and fluffy. When there is no sweetener around to eat, yeasts become inactive and spring to life again when conditions are favorable.